Original title:
Tea, Tides, and Cozy Times

Copyright © 2024 Creative Arts Management OÜ
All rights reserved.

Author: Dexter Sullivan
ISBN HARDBACK: 978-9916-94-450-9
ISBN PAPERBACK: 978-9916-94-451-6

Whispers in a Cup

Steam rises softly, whispers of warmth,
A cozy embrace, like a gentle charm.
In porcelain vessels, stories unfold,
Moments cherished, secrets told.

Rustling leaves sing their quiet song,
In this sanctuary, where hearts belong.
With every sip, our spirits align,
In every flavor, a spark divine.

Gentle Waves of Comfort

Soft tides brush against the shore,
Whispers of peace, forevermore.
In soothing hues of blue and green,
Nature's embrace, a love unseen.

Each wave a promise, a calming sigh,
Under the vast and endless sky.
A dance of comfort, pure and free,
The rhythm of life, a symphony.

Sips Beneath the Stars

Starlit skies, a canvas bright,
We gather close, hearts alight.
With every sip, we dream and soar,
The universe whispers, forevermore.

Constellations twinkle, stories unfold,
In every glance, a world to hold.
A tapestry woven with wishes and dreams,
In warmth and laughter, hope redeems.

Currents of Warmth

Embers flicker, shadows dance,
In this glow, we take our chance.
The fire crackles, tales arise,
Binding us with summer skies.

Warmth flowing, hearts entwined,
In this moment, love aligned.
The essence of life, pure and true,
In every heartbeat, me and you.

Moments Adrift in Time

Silent whispers weave through the years,
Fleeting joys behind veil of tears.
Forgotten dreams, like leaves they fall,
Drifting softly, answering the call.

Each heartbeat echoes a tender voice,
Woven threads of fate, no choice.
In twilight's dance, we let time bend,
Embracing the moments that never end.

Lush Landscapes and Warm Embraces

Where rolling hills touch the skies,
Colors dance as daylight flies.
In the arms of nature, we find peace,
As every worry begins to cease.

With laughter shared beneath the trees,
Soft whispers carried by the breeze.
In lush landscapes, hearts embrace,
Finding joy in every place.

The Flavor of Faltering Light

Sunset drips in hues so bold,
Stories of the day unfold.
Fingers trace the fading glow,
Capturing all that we know.

With twilight's kiss, the world draws near,
A taste of time, a hint of fear.
In the dimming light, we find our way,
As shadows dance, they softly sway.

Soothing Touch of the Gulf

Gentle waves caress the shore,
Whispers of the sea, a calming roar.
Sun-kissed sands beneath our feet,
Nature's rhythm, a pulse so sweet.

In salty air, we breathe in deep,
Finding solace where secrets keep.
The gulf's embrace, a tender sigh,
Lifts our spirits as we fly.

The Scroll of the Sea

Whispers of waves on golden sands,
Ancient tales in salty hands.
Each tide brings secrets untold,
In the deep blue, a treasure unfolds.

A sailor's heart, wide and free,
Guided by stars, the map of the sea.
Songs of the ocean, wild and grand,
Echo through time, across the land.

Quietude in Each Brew

In the stillness, a kettle hums,
A dance of steam as the quiet comes.
Leaves unfold in a gentle embrace,
Sipping solace, finding grace.

Each cup tells stories of sunlit days,
Of whispered dreams in a fragrant haze.
A moment paused, the world in check,
In every sip, the heart's trek.

A Journey of Flavors and Waves

Drifting on a breeze, spices align,
A voyage begins with each taste divine.
From shores of salt to fields of grain,
A blend of life, joy, and pain.

Layers unfold with passion and art,
Each flavor carries the map of the heart.
An adventure awaits within each bite,
Truth in the savor, pure delight.

Opening Up to Nature's Sips

Among the trees, where silence sings,
Nature's bounty, a gift that clings.
Water from springs, pure and bright,
Quenching souls in the fading light.

Petals steeped in morning's dew,
With every sip, the world feels new.
A journey unfolds beneath the sky,
In nature's embrace, we learn to fly.

Ripples of Comfort

In gentle waves the whispers call,
Soothing hearts, they rise and fall.
Each ripple brings a soft embrace,
A tranquil touch, a sacred space.

The worries fade, the mind finds peace,
As currents flow, our fears release.
In every splash, a story shared,
In water's dance, we feel repaired.

The sunlight shimmers on the lake,
With every breath, we start to wake.
The gentle sound, a lullaby,
In ripples soft, our spirits fly.

Sheltered from the Storm

Beneath the roof, the winds may howl,
Yet here, we bask, away from growl.
The rain may fall, but we are dry,
With love and warmth, we gently sigh.

The thunder cracks, the shadows loom,
But in this space, there's hope to bloom.
With every heartbeat, we draw close,
In shared delight, our hearts engross.

The tempest roars beyond our door,
Yet here we find an endless shore.
Together safe, we weave our dreams,
In whispered prayers, the silence gleams.

Embracing Nature's Lullaby

In rustling leaves, a song is spun,
A melody 'neath the setting sun.
The river hums a soothing tune,
As night descends, we dance with moon.

The stars will twinkle, soft and bright,
In nature's arms, we find our light.
Each creature sings, a gentle sound,
In harmony, our souls are bound.

The branches sway, a whispered prayer,
In every breeze, we find our care.
With open hearts, the world we greet,
In nature's lullaby, we sleep.

Brewed Memories upon the Shore

With every sip, a tale unfolds,
In fragrant steam, our life beholds.
The ocean's whispers blend with tea,
As waves dance close, we roam set free.

The sun dips low, we trace the sand,
With laughter shared, we hand in hand.
Each moment sipped, a story told,
Brewed memories in colors bold.

The taste of salt, the warmth of brew,
Together here, the world feels new.
As twilight sings, we cling to time,
In our embrace, the stars will chime.

Embraced by Flavor and the Sea

Waves whisper secrets to the shore,
Tasting salt where the seagulls soar.
Fruits of the ocean dance on the plate,
A symphony of warmth, it's never too late.

Savor the moments as they unfold,
Each bite a story waiting to be told.
Sunset hues blend in a vibrant spread,
As laughter mingles with fish and bread.

The breeze carries flavors, bold and bright,
Under the canvas of fading light.
Every dish a memory, oh so sweet,
In the heart of the sea, life feels complete.

Embraced by flavors, we wander free,
Lost in the magic of you and me.
Together we feast on what's fresh and true,
As the ocean's heartbeat lulls us anew.

Savoring Stillness in the Air

In the quiet dawn, I breathe anew,
Golden light kisses the morning dew.
A moment lingered, time stands still,
In this serene space, I find my will.

Birds are singing, a gentle refrain,
Nature's chorus, free from pain.
Each note a blessing, soft and clear,
I savor the silence, draw you near.

With every whisper of the cool air,
My spirit dances, shedding despair.
Life unfurls like petals in bloom,
In this calm haven, I find my room.

Savoring stillness, a treasure so rare,
Moments like these, beyond compare.
Under the sky's embrace, I awake,
In tranquil layers, my heart will quake.

The Art of Quiet Reflection

In the stillness, thoughts arise,
Whispers of dreams beneath the skies.
A canvas blank, with colors bright,
Painting my heart in soft twilight.

Hushed moments hold the truth I seek,
In gentle whispers, silence speaks.
Each breath a note in the symphony,
Inviting me to just simply be.

With every glance at the mirror's light,
I find solace in the starry night.
The art of reflection, a sacred space,
Where worries dissolve, and fears embrace.

Quietly I ponder, let shadows pass,
Inward journeys, like ripples of glass.
With open arms, I learn to see,
The beauty that lies within me.

Currents of Calm and Flavor

In the heart of the river, time flows slow,
Currents of calm, where soft breezes blow.
Flavors of nature, ripe on the vine,
Whispers of fruits, sweet and divine.

Each droplet dances on the water's face,
Embracing the sun in a warm embrace.
Savoring moments, rich and profound,
In the tranquility, peace can be found.

As shadows stretch under the willow's shade,
The melody of life in me is played.
Currents of flavor, tide of the day,
Together we linger, forever we stay.

On this journey, where senses unite,
Each taste a story, each sound a flight.
Currents of calm, flavors we weave,
In the serenity of nature, I believe.

Echoes of Steam and Sand

Whispers of heat rise and dance,
Grains of time slip through like chance.
Footsteps trail where shadows blend,
In the silence, journeys mend.

Steam swirls softly, tales unfold,
Memories wrapped in warmth of gold.
Sand beneath, a timeless friend,
Echoes linger; they never end.

Waves will crash with every tide,
In this world where dreams reside.
Chasing whispers, lost and found,
Life's sweet cadence, a gentle sound.

Each grain's story, soft and grand,
Breathe in deeply, understand.
Moments held in steam and sand,
In this dance, we take our stand.

Infusions of Comfort and Joy

A steaming cup held in warm hands,
Cardamom scent softly expands.
With every sip, the heart will sing,
Joyful warmth that memories bring.

Spices swirled in a tender blend,
Laughter lingers around the bend.
In cozy corners, love does flow,
Infusions deep where spirits glow.

Cinnamon whispers, sweet delight,
Every drop a perfect bite.
Comfort settles like a safe embrace,
In this moment, we find our place.

Together, we chase the worries away,
Savoring warmth in the light of day.
With each infusion, hearts unite,
A dance of joy, pure and bright.

Sunlit Serenity in Every Drop

Morning breaks with golden light,
Every drop a spark, so bright.
Nature's gift in crystal form,
Serenity wrapped in the warm.

Sunlight dances on the stream,
Every ripple a gentle dream.
Time slows down in this embrace,
Life reflected, a tender grace.

Gentle breezes carry whispers,
In this hush, the heart lingers.
Moments captured, sweet and pure,
Sunlit solace, a perfect cure.

Every drop tells a story,
Filling spaces with transient glory.
Breathe in deep, feel the flow,
In nature's arms, we gently grow.

Harboring Warmth in Chilly Winds

Beneath the storm, a refuge stands,
Holding tight with steady hands.
In the chill, a fire glows,
Whispers comfort, love bestows.

Winds may howl, the world may sway,
Yet in here, we'll find our way.
Blankets wrapped, we share a smile,
Time together, all worthwhile.

Snowflakes dance in wild delight,
Yet our hearts remain so bright.
Glowing embers, stories shared,
In this warmth, we know we've cared.

Winter's grip can't chill our bond,
With every laugh, our hearts respond.
In the harbor of laughter and light,
We conquer darkness, shining bright.

Chasing Clouds with Warmth

Through skies of blue, we run and play,
Chasing clouds that drift away.
Laughter echoes, light and free,
In this world, just you and me.

The sunbeams wrap us in their glow,
Guiding pathways we both know.
With every step, our spirits rise,
Chasing dreams across the skies.

An Ocean of Solace

Waves caress the golden shore,
Whispers of peace forevermore.
Salted air and sandy feet,
At this haven, hearts can meet.

The tides bring tales from far away,
As seabirds dance at the break of day.
In every splash, a story flows,
An ocean's love forever grows.

Cozy Corners under the Stars

In cozy nooks where shadows play,
We find our warmth at close of day.
Stars above begin to gleam,
While whispers drift like a gentle dream.

Soft blankets wrap us, side by side,
In this space, our hearts confide.
Every twinkle holds a secret,
In our corner, joy's our ticket.

Tender Moments in a Salted Breeze

The breeze carries scents of the sea,
In tender moments, just you and me.
With hearts that sway like the gentle tide,
We cherish the warmth where love can hide.

Beneath the sky, painted in gold,
Each glance shared, a story told.
Time slows down in this embrace,
In salty air, we find our place.

A Sip of Bliss by the Fire

The flames dance bright, a warm embrace,
A steaming mug in a quiet space.
Whispers of joy in the crackling sound,
A sip of bliss where peace is found.

Golden hues flicker, shadows play,
Moments of stillness in a calming sway.
With every taste, the worries flee,
By the fire's glow, just you and me.

Gentle Cradles of Flavor

Whispers of spice in the evening air,
Softly cradled with flavors rare.
Delicate notes in a tender dance,
A culinary dream, a chance romance.

Each bite, a treasure, each sip, a song,
Together we savor, where we belong.
Moments woven with laughter and cheer,
Gentle cradles, warmth drawing near.

Resting in the Embrace of Nature

Soft petals fall in a sunlit haze,
Nature whispers secrets in gentle ways.
Beneath tall trees, in a quiet glade,
Resting in beauty, memories made.

Rustling leaves and the call of birds,
A symphony sung without any words.
Time stands still, in this sacred space,
Nature's embrace, a pure, sweet grace.

The Aroma of Salty Skies

Waves crash softly on the sun-warmed shore,
The sea breeze whispers, a familiar lore.
Salty skies cradle the dreams we find,
In every gust, a fleeting mind.

Footprints in sand tell stories untold,
Moments of wonder, forever bold.
With salty air and hearts open wide,
The ocean's love, our constant guide.

Sips of Serenity

In the quiet of dawn,
A cup warms my hands.
Easing the night away,
With each soft sip I take.

Flavors dance on my tongue,
Spices of earth and sky.
Moments linger softly,
As whispers fill the air.

Sunrise paints the horizon,
Colors blend and unfold.
Serenity envelops,
Like a blanket of gold.

In this tranquil stillness,
Time slows to a crawl.
The world fades around me,
With each sip, I am whole.

The Comfort of Warm Waters

Beneath a sky so vast,
The waters cradle me.
Ripples kiss my skin,
In a gentle, sweet embrace.

Steam rises like dreams,
Carrying worries away.
In the comfort of warmth,
I find my heart's true peace.

Waves whisper soft secrets,
In a language of their own.
Together we breathe slowly,
In this moment, I am home.

A sanctuary awaits,
In the depths of the blue.
With every splash that lingers,
The world feels fresh and new.

Gentle Swells and Soothing Brews

The ocean breathes with grace,
Waves break against the shore.
Each swell brings a promise,
Of calm and of warmth once more.

Teas brewed with care, so fine,
Pouring solace in a cup.
Every sip is a journey,
As the world stirs and stirs up.

Sunset casts its soft glow,
On waters deep and wide.
In these gentle moments,
I lose myself inside.

For in swells and brews I find,
The rhythm of my soul.
Finding peace in each drop,
As I let the waves roll.

Mornings Wrapped in Warmth

Mornings break like soft folds,
Sunlight dances on the pane.
Wrapped in cozy blankets,
I embrace life's gentle refrain.

A cup of warmth beside me,
Comfort lingers in the air.
Each sip a sweet reminder,
Of the love that's always there.

Birds chirp their morning songs,
Nature wakes with a sigh.
In this moment, I am still,
Underneath the vast wide sky.

Days begin with hope's whisper,
And joy in simple things.
Wrapped in warmth, I cherish,
The beauty that each day brings.

Splashing Colors of Comfort

In a world of vibrant hues,
Joyful splashes paint the day.
Warmth of laughter fills the air,
Comfort in the colors play.

Soft pastels and bold delights,
Embrace the heart and soul.
Every stroke a gentle touch,
Making broken pieces whole.

From deep indigos to sunlit yellows,
Each shade a story to tell.
In the canvas of our lives,
Every color casts its spell.

So let the palette come alive,
With love, let worries cease.
In splashing colors, we will find,
A blissful, vibrant peace.

Lullabies of the Shore

Gentle waves caress the sand,
Whispers of the sea's embrace.
A lullaby from nature's hand,
Bringing calm to every space.

Moonlit tides, a silver glow,
Seashells sing a soft refrain.
In the night, the breezes blow,
Washing worries down the drain.

Crickets chirp and stars align,
The ocean hums a tender tune.
With every breath, the heart entwines,
Underneath the watchful moon.

Here at the edge of dreams and wake,
In this serenity we dwell.
Lullabies of the shore, they make
A soothing, sacred spell.

Holding Space in a Cozy Nook

In a corner wrapped in light,
Soft pillows call my name.
A cozy nook, a pure delight,
Where peace and warmth reclaim.

With a book in hand, I dive,
Into worlds both vast and bright.
Here, in solitude, I thrive,
As time flows gentle and light.

A steaming cup beside my side,
Whispers of a world outside.
In the stillness, I confide,
As dreams and thoughts abide.

Holding space, my spirit soars,
Wrapped in comfort, soft and true.
Here in my nook, my heart explores,
The beauty found in quiet hue.

Flowing Spirits at Dusk

As daylight fades to shades of gold,
The sky ignites in twilight's grace.
Whispers of secrets yet untold,
Dance like shadows in this space.

Winds carry stories from afar,
To blend with dusk's enchanting glow.
Here, beneath the first bright star,
Our flowing spirits start to grow.

Colors merge in a soft embrace,
As night unfolds its velvet veil.
In this fleeting magic place,
We weave the night, a wondrous tale.

Let dreams and hopes take flight tonight,
In harmony with the fading light.
Flowing spirits, free and bright,
In the dusk, we feel delight.

In the Arms of the Waves

The waves embrace the shore,
Whispers of the ocean's roar,
Glistening under the sun,
Nature's dance has just begun.

A salty breeze begins to play,
Carrying worries far away,
Each ebb and flow, so divine,
In each crash, a story entwined.

Footprints washed with every tide,
Secrets in the depths abide,
Chasing dreams beneath the sky,
In the arms of waves, we fly.

Melodies in the Cup

Steam curls in the morning light,
A fragrant brew, a pure delight,
Each sip sings a soothing song,
In the heart, where we belong.

Cinnamon and clove entwined,
Whispers of comfort, sweet and kind,
Moments pause in every taste,
Time slows down, no need for haste.

In porcelain, warmth does reside,
A simple joy, a gentle guide,
Melodies linger, soft and sweet,
In every cup, our dreams repeat.

Quiet Reflections on a Sandy Shore

Footsteps trace the shoreline's edge,
Mirrored thoughts in the water's pledge,
Glimmers dance where the waves retreat,
A tranquil space where heartbeats meet.

Seagulls cry, the sun stands tall,
Nature's harmony, embracing all,
Shells whisper stories from the deep,
In soft embraces, I find peace.

The world fades with the setting sun,
Quiet moments, two become one,
Under stars, the night's allure,
In this stillness, we feel secure.

Brews of Contentment

A kettle sings a soothing note,
Beneath the stars, our dreams afloat,
Herbal warmth in every cup,
In simple moments, we fill up.

Laughter shared like fragrant steam,
Worries fade; they are but dreams,
With every sip, a pause to feel,
In every heart, a gentle heal.

The world outside may rush and fly,
Here, we linger, just you and I,
In brews of warmth, we find our way,
Contentment flows, come what may.

Serene Blends at Twilight

The sky blushes as day departs,
Stars emerge like whispered arts.
Gentle hues collide and dance,
In twilight's calm, we take a chance.

Soft whispers sway the evening air,
Cool breezes weave without a care.
The world slows down, the heart finds peace,
In this moment, all tensions cease.

The shadows stretch, the night grows deep,
In tranquil thoughts, our minds can leap.
Nature's palette, painted bright,
Fades into the velvet night.

As silence wraps the earth in grace,
We find solace in this place.
With every breath, serenity blends,
In twilight's grip, our spirit mends.

Waves of Tranquility

Softly crashing on the shore,
Waves whisper secrets, tales of yore.
Each ebb and flow, a calming song,
In their embrace, we all belong.

The sun dips low, casts golden rays,
Painting the sea in twilight's blaze.
Each ripple stirs the sands of time,
In this stillness, hearts can rhyme.

Seagulls soar in the gentle breeze,
Nature's beauty, a moment to seize.
With salt-kissed air, we close our eyes,
Finding peace beneath wide skies.

In the distance, horizons blend,
Where sky and water softly mend.
In waves of calm, worries fall away,
Embracing night, welcoming day.

The Elixir of Peace

A quiet cup, the steam ascends,
In this moment, the heart transcends.
Warmth envelops my weary hands,
In solitude, my spirit stands.

Each sip, a journey to the soul,
As flavors swirl, I feel whole.
The world outside may rush and race,
But here within, I find my place.

The gentle clink of porcelain fine,
A tranquil space where thoughts align.
As steam dissolves in evening light,
I breathe in calm, release the night.

In every drop, a tale unfolds,
Of silent dreams and wisdom old.
The elixir of peace, it flows so free,
A cherished mug, just me and me.

Curling Steam and Soft Breezes

In the morning light, steam curls high,
A dance of warmth, as time drifts by.
Each breath brings comfort, soft and keen,
In gentle moments, the world is seen.

Outside, the breeze whispers low,
Embracing petals, making them glow.
Nature's kiss, a tender grace,
In this stillness, we find our place.

A fragrant blend, the air so sweet,
With every heartbeat, we feel complete.
As steam rises with the dawn's embrace,
We celebrate life's elegant pace.

In quiet mornings, we softly sway,
With curling steam, we greet the day.
The softest breezes, a soothing balm,
In nature's arms, we find our calm.

Moments Between the Drops

Raindrops dance on window panes,
Whispers of a soft refrain.
Time slows to a gentle hush,
In the heart, the memories rush.

Each droplet tells a tale anew,
Of laughter shared, of skies so blue.
A fleeting glance, a secret sigh,
In pauses found, the moments lie.

Underneath the silver skies,
Footsteps fade where silence lies.
In the stillness, dreams take flight,
Moments cradle soft twilight.

Between the drops, we find our space,
In every tear, a trace of grace.
Life's rhythm beats, a tender thrum,
In the quietude, we become.

Ebb and Flow of Heartfelt Brews

In the cup, a warmth so deep,
A comfort found, a love to keep.
Sipping slowly, world outside,
With every taste, the heart's divide.

Cinnamon dreams and vanilla skies,
Brews that hide beneath the sighs.
Stirring thoughts, like leaves in air,
Each flavor whispers, none to spare.

The steam rises, a soft embrace,
In every drop, we find our place.
Brewing stories, shared at dusk,
In every sip, an endless trust.

Ebb and flow of joy and pain,
Through every drink, we bear the strain.
In porcelain warmth, our spirits blend,
Heartfelt brews that transcend.

Fables of the Horizon

Every sunrise tells a tale,
Upon the winds, the whispers sail.
Colors meld in morning's light,
Chasing dreams into the night.

Waves crashing on invisible shores,
Fables written in nature's score.
Horizons stretch beyond the eye,
In the distance, secrets lie.

Stars awaken as dusk unfolds,
Stories whispered, truths retold.
Each twinkle holds a history,
In dreams we're bound, we'll always be.

From shadows cast, new paths are drawn,
In the fables, we are reborn.
A journey etched in time's own sail,
Where every spirit leaves a trail.

Warmth Cradled in Porcelain

Morning sunlight softly glows,
A sacred space where stillness flows.
Warmed by tea in gentle hands,
In this moment, time expands.

Porcelain cups like fragile dreams,
Holding whispers, holding beams.
With each sip, our worries cease,
In simple acts, we find our peace.

The world outside fades into shades,
As conversation quietly pervades.
Laughter dances with fragrant scents,
In these moments, life's content.

Cradled warmth, a loving brew,
In every heartbeat, made anew.
Porcelain holds our cherished time,
In its embrace, we softly rhyme.

Mellow Brews and Gentle Shores

On shores where whispers meet the sea,
The sun dips low, so warm and free.
A gentle breeze, a silken sigh,
Where dreams drift softly, like birds that fly.

With every sip of mellow brew,
The evening sky turns shades of blue.
Reflections dance on waters bright,
As stars awaken, one by one, at night.

The Rhythm of Rest

In quiet corners, time stands still,
The heartbeats sync, the world is chill.
Let burdens fade with evening glow,
As tranquil moments gently flow.

A sigh released, the day flows out,
In dreams we wander, free of doubt.
The rhythm of rest, a sweet embrace,
In slumber's arms, we find our place.

Flickering Lights and Brews

Underneath the stars so bright,
Flickering lights bring warmth and sight.
With every lift of cups we share,
Our laughter mingles in the air.

The night's a canvas, painted bold,
With stories shared and secrets told.
A cozy corner, hearts aligned,
In this sweetness, solace we find.

Sand Between Toes and Sweetness in Hand

With grains of sand that kiss our feet,
We walk along where land and sea meet.
The sweetness of sun-kissed clime,
Echoes softly, like a verse in rhyme.

In breezy whispers, joy expands,
Life's little treasures, soft in our hands.
As waves unfold, our laughter flows,
In moments fleeting, our spirit grows.

Invocations of Solace

In the hush of dawn's embrace,
Whispers of peace find their place.
Gentle dreams in the morning light,
Soulful shadows take their flight.

Through the trees, a soft refrain,
Calling hearts to shed their pain.
Moonlit paths and silver streams,
Invoke the quiet of our dreams.

With each breath, the world unwinds,
Leaving behind the ties that bind.
In still moments, solace grows,
Like a flower, beauty shows.

In the evening's tender grace,
We find our thoughts, our sacred space.
Echoes of love in every tone,
Every heart will find its home.

Timeless Cozy Conversations

Beneath a quilt of stars so bright,
We gather close, igniting light.
Stories shared, laughter rings,
In this warmth, our spirit sings.

With spoken words, the night unfolds,
Embracing dreams that never grow old.
Time stands still, as memories blend,
In cozy chats, hearts mend.

Each sip we take, a moment savored,
In whispered tones, love is favored.
Through every tale, we find our way,
In timeless bonds, we choose to stay.

Though days may pass and seasons change,
In our hearts, we'll never range.
For cozy talks and friendship's grace,
Are treasures time can't erase.

Secrets from the Kettle

Steam rises with a gentle sigh,
Songs of warmth begin to fly.
In the kettle's soothing hum,
Ancient secrets start to drum.

Herbs and spices dance with glee,
Infusing dreams that set us free.
Each swirl whispers tales untold,
Liquid magic, bright and bold.

From chamomile to ginger's fire,
Each brew ignites a deep desire.
In the swirl of colors bright,
Memories linger, pure delight.

Pouring forth, the essence flows,
With every cup, our spirit grows.
Together we sip, together we find,
Secrets shared, our hearts aligned.

Evening Hues and Gentle Brews

As the sun sinks low and fades,
Nighttime's curtain softly cascades.
Colors blend in softest sighs,
Painting dreams across the skies.

With each brew, the day unwinds,
Sipping slowly, peace we find.
In twilight's glow, our hearts align,
Feeling the pulse of the divine.

Whispers of dusk in every cup,
Stirring souls, lifting us up.
Embracing warmth, the world feels right,
In gentle brews and fading light.

The evening wraps us in its care,
With every moment, love will share.
Together in this timeless flow,
Two hearts beat soft, understated glow.

Salty Air and Silken Comfort

The waves crash softly on the shore,
A breeze that whispers tales of yore.
Sunsets paint the sky in gold,
In this embrace, our hearts unfold.

Fingers entwined, we stroll along,
To the rhythm of nature's song.
The salty air, a gentle kiss,
In a moment, we find our bliss.

Seagulls dive and laugh with glee,
As if to share their joy with me.
Each breath a treasure, fresh and new,
In this ocean's arms, love feels true.

The night descends, stars start to gleam,
Wrapped in comfort, we softly dream.
In salty air, our spirits soar,
Together forever, we seek no more.

Misty Mornings with a Warm Embrace

Fog blankets the world in white,
A soothing pause before the light.
With coffee steaming in our hands,
We wander through soft, silent lands.

The sun peeks through the drifting mist,
In this moment, we can't resist.
Each step is calm, a gentle sway,
In nature's hug, we'll find our way.

Birds begin their morning calls,
Echoing through the quiet halls.
Whispers of the dawn arrive,
In this stillness, we come alive.

Together wrapped in warmth and cheer,
Every shared glance drawing us near.
Misty mornings guide us home,
In this serenity, we freely roam.

A Pot of Calm

In a corner sits a pot of tea,
Brewing warmth and harmony.
Leaves unfurl in fragrant steam,
Each sip a moment, a cherished dream.

Quiet clinks of cups align,
As time slows down and hearts entwine.
The world outside fades away,
In this embrace, we choose to stay.

Sunlight streams through window panes,
Dancing shadows, casting lanes.
Within this space, troubles cease,
A pot of calm, a cup of peace.

We share our thoughts, our laughs, our sighs,
In every moment, love complies.
Here in this sanctuary, we belong,
With every heartbeat, we grow strong.

Toasting to Stillness

Raise your glass to the quiet night,
To the stars that shimmer bright.
In the stillness, we find our grace,
In gentle moments, we leave a trace.

The world fades into shadows deep,
As we savor memories to keep.
With every laugh, our spirits lift,
In gratitude, we share this gift.

The fire crackles, warmth surrounds,
In this haven, love abounds.
Let's toast to peace, to dreams that last,
In the present, forgetting the past.

Together in this sacred space,
Finding joy in every face.
Toasting to stillness, hearts in tune,
Under the banner of the moon.

Driftwood Dreams and Elixirs

Driftwood rests upon the shore,
Whispers of the ocean's roar.
Ebbing tides in twilight's glow,
Dreams adrift in ebb and flow.

Chasing stars in moonlit skies,
Elixirs bright, where magic lies.
Sipping tales of days gone by,
In the silence, we learn to fly.

With each wave, old secrets call,
Carved by time, they rise and fall.
In the breeze, forgotten lore,
Driftwood dreams, forevermore.

Captured in this fleeting dance,
Life's sweet moments, a second chance.
In every glass, our spirits blend,
A journey shared, until the end.

Moments Wrapped in Steam

Morning light through frosted glass,
Steam curls up, a gentle pass.
Moments wrapped in warmth and care,
Nature speaks with whispered air.

Tea brews softly, aromas rise,
Memories linger, no goodbyes.
In each sip, a story told,
Moments wrapped in warmth, pure gold.

Outside, the chill, the frostbite's grip,
Inside, a cozy, timeless trip.
Steam embraces, shadows play,
In this warmth, we wish to stay.

Ovens crackle, dough will rise,
Sharing laughter, gentle sighs.
Wrapped in steam, we're never far,
In this haven, love's the star.

Nachos with Warmth and Whispers

Crunchy bites in evening light,
Nachos shared, a pure delight.
Cheese drips down, warm and rich,
Every flavor, a cozy niche.

Spice and laughter fill the air,
Whispers soft in joyful care.
Salsa dances on every chip,
A melting taste, a perfect sip.

Families gather, friends unite,
Hearts entwined in this warm night.
With every bite, stories flow,
Nachos shared, the love will grow.

Under stars, the moon takes flight,
Together, everything feels right.
In warmth and whispers, we reside,
With nachos close, and hearts open wide.

A Slow Dance with the Horizon

At dusk, the colors start to blend,
A slow dance as day meets end.
Golden hues in twilight's grasp,
Nature's hand, a gentle clasp.

Clouds drift lazily in the sky,
Whispers of dreams that float on high.
Each moment stretches, time stands still,
In the embrace of peace, we feel.

The ocean mirrors the fading light,
Soft waves whisper, day turns to night.
Together, we sway with grace,
In this dance, we find our place.

Hand in hand, we trace the line,
Between the stars, love's design.
A slow dance with the horizon wide,
In this stillness, we will abide.

Driftwood Dreams

On the shore where whispers rest,
Driftwood lies, a weary guest.
Fragments of the sea's embrace,
Carved by time, no secret's trace.

Waves echo tales of distant lands,
Where the sun meets golden sands.
In the silence, dreams take flight,
Guided by the fading light.

Pieces of a story spun,
Of the moon and of the sun.
Nature's art on ocean's weave,
In each form, the heart believes.

Through the hours, shadows sway,
Driftwood sings of yesterday.
A reminder in the sand,
Of the journeys that were planned.

Floral Notes

In the garden, colors blend,
Petals dance, the breezes send.
Fragrant whispers fill the air,
Nature's symphony laid bare.

Bees will hum their busy tune,
Underneath the watchful moon.
Every bloom, a story told,
In their hearts, the warmth of gold.

Sunlight kisses every stem,
Painting life, a vibrant gem.
Each bud holds a dream to share,
Music woven everywhere.

From the roots to skies above,
Floral notes of peace and love.
Celebrate the fleeting sight,
In their beauty, pure delight.

The Choicest Moments at Dusk

As the day begins to fade,
Golden hues begin to braid.
Whispers soft as shadows grow,
Time pauses, moods ebb and flow.

Crickets chirp their evening song,
While the stars are pulled along.
Every breath, a gentle sigh,
Underneath the velvet sky.

Twilight paints the world anew,
In shades of pink and deepest blue.
A fleeting hush, a sacred space,
Captured in this soft embrace.

Moments linger, hearts entwined,
In the dusk, true beauty find.
As the night begins to hum,
Soft reminders, love will come.

Nature's Brew in Heartbeats

In the forest, life unfolds,
Whispers of the earth retold.
Beneath the canopy so wide,
Nature's brew, an endless tide.

Roots entwined in secret dance,
Every leaf, a second chance.
Beating hearts in harmony,
Strumming chords of memory.

Mossy carpets, cool and green,
Shelter for the unseen.
Echoes of a world alive,
In this space, our spirits thrive.

Breath of wind, a gentle guide,
Through the wild, we shall abide.
In each moment, magic stirs,
Nature's song, the heart concurs.

Raindrops and Revelations

Softly falls the silver rain,
Whispers soothing every pain.
Raindrops kiss the thirsty ground,
In their dance, so sweet, profound.

Each droplet tells a secret tale,
Of distant clouds and journeys frail.
Nature's tears bring life anew,
For every heart, for every hue.

Amidst the showers, thoughts arise,
Reflections spark beneath the skies.
Cleansed by water, spirits rise,
In the rain, a love that ties.

With every splash, a revelation,
A moment's calm, a celebration.
Through the storm, we find our way,
Raindrops linger, hearts will sway.

Savoring Slow Moments

In quiet time, we linger long,
As shadows stretch, we hum our song.
The world outside, it fades away,
In stillness, joy finds light of day.

A cup of tea, a book in hand,
We weave our dreams like grains of sand.
The ticking clock cannot be heard,
In gentle peace, our hearts are stirred.

The whispers of the evening breeze,
Remind us to take time with ease.
With every breath, we find our ground,
In moments slow, true love is found.

So let us pause this hectic race,
To find our calm, to find our place.
In savoring, our souls will blend,
With every sigh, our spirits mend.

Chasing the Setting Sun

We run against the golden light,
With laughter loud, our hearts take flight.
The sky ignites in hues so bold,
As day gives way to dreams untold.

With open arms, we greet the dusk,
In every shimmer, every husk.
The sun dips low, a fiery kiss,
In twilight's glow, we find our bliss.

Across the hills, the shadows creep,
While secrets of the night we keep.
Together, we embrace the night,
In chasing dusk, we find our light.

So let us wander, hand in hand,
Into the shades of evening's land.
For in this chase, our spirits run,
Through hues of red, we've just begun.

Sailboats and Sweetness

Sailboats dance on ocean's crest,
With whispers soft, they find their rest.
The tide pulls gently, waves that sing,
A melody of summer's fling.

With sun-kissed skin, we cast away,
Our dreams afloat on bright array.
Each gust of wind a sweet caress,
In motion's grace, our souls undress.

The horizon calls, a endless quest,
To chase the waves that never rest.
With laughter shared, we chart our course,
In sails of love, we find our source.

As stars emerge, we drop our fears,
The night enfolds, a warmth that steers.
In sailboats bold, we set our dreams,
In sweet pursuits, life's treasure gleams.

Warmth in the Winds

Beneath the trees, the breezes sigh,
As whispers blend with songs nearby.
With every gust, a gentle touch,
In nature's breath, we find so much.

The golden rays of sunbeam's friend,
Bring warmth and cheer that seems to mend.
As autumn leaves begin to twirl,
In every swirl, our hearts unfurl.

The laughter carried on the air,
Reminds us all that life is rare.
With arms outstretched, we feel the grace,
In wind's embrace, we find our space.

So let us dance and spin with glee,
In every gust, we feel so free.
For warmth in winds, a sweet caress,
In nature's song, our souls find rest.

Footprints in the Sand

Upon the shore, where oceans gleam,
Footprints tell of love's sweet dream.
Waves rush in and gently erase,
Memories held in time and space.

Each grain of sand, a story told,
Of journeys taken, brave and bold.
In twilight's glow, they softly fade,
Yet in the heart, they'll ne'er evade.

With every step, a silent plea,
To hold the past, to set it free.
The tide may change, the winds may blow,
But in my heart, your essence flows.

As stars appear in evening's hue,
I walk this path, remembering you.
Though footprints fade, the love remains,
A bond unbroken, free from chains.

A Palette of Comfort and Chill

In chilly air, the colors blend,
Soft sweaters drape, and warmth they send.
Leaves turn gold, then dance and sway,
In autumn's arms, they find their way.

Cinnamon wafts from cozy nooks,
Hot cider waits in simple looks.
By the fire, tales intertwine,
A palette rich, where hearts align.

Misty mornings greet the dawn,
In nature's arms, where dreams are drawn.
With every breath, a chill we embrace,
And comfort found in a warm space.

Together we weave through golden trails,
In laughter's echo, love never fails.
In the heart of fall, we find our peace,
A palette of comfort that will not cease.

Melodies of the Evening Breeze

The evening breeze begins to sing,
With whispers soft, its magic brings.
Stars awaken, the sky's a stage,
In twilight's glow, we turn the page.

Crickets chirp their secret tune,
As fireflies dance beneath the moon.
A symphony from nature's core,
Invites our hearts to feel the score.

Each gentle gust carries a wish,
A fleeting thought, a fleeting kiss.
In shadows deep, where silence dwells,
The breeze entwines with untold spells.

Moments linger, the night unfolds,
A story of dreams, both new and old.
In melodies where love appears,
The evening breeze calms all our fears.

Shadows and Solace

In quiet corners, shadows creep,
They weave their tales while others sleep.
A soft embrace of dark and light,
Where solace finds us in the night.

The moonlight bathes the world in glow,
As whispers rise from depths below.
In solitude, we learn to see,
That shadows hold a part of me.

Beneath the weight of silence deep,
Awakens thoughts that gently seep.
With every breath, a chance to heal,
The solace found, the heart can feel.

For in the shadows, truth prevails,
A gentle hand through life's travails.
So let the night draw near and call,
In shadows' arms, we rise, we fall.

Quietude by the Shore

Waves softly crash on sand,
In a dance, they breathe and sigh.
Seagulls call from skies so grand,
Beneath the vast and azure sky.

Footprints fade with each retreat,
Gentle whispers through the breeze.
Salted air and time repeat,
Nature's song puts the soul at ease.

Driftwood stories, ancient lore,
Lulled by tides that ebb and flow.
In this peace, I seek no more,
Just the sun's warm, golden glow.

Moments linger, hearts align,
In the hush, we find our place.
Lost in thoughts, your hand in mine,
Quietude, a sweet embrace.

Reflections in a Warm Glass

A drink adorned with glimmers bright,
The amber liquid slowly swirls.
In stillness, thoughts take flight,
As memories dance and twirl.

Rumors of laughter float along,
Echoes of joy entwined with strife.
In each sip, a whispered song,
Bringing warmth to this fragile life.

Each clink of glass, a toast to fate,
To dreams we hold and chase in vain.
A simple drink, yet so ornate,
Within its depths, both grief and gain.

With friends beside, we share the night,
Reflections shimmer in our eyes.
In this moment, all feels right,
As stars awaken in the skies.

Whispers in the Brew

Steam rises from the porcelain cup,
A scent so rich, it fills the air.
Quiet murmurs, sup by sup,
In morning's light, without a care.

The world awakes, a gentle hum,
Soft notes of life begin to play.
In every sip, the heartbeats drum,
Stirring dreams at dawn's ballet.

Cinnamon hints, a dash of hope,
In liquid warmth, we find our way.
With every brew, we learn to cope,
Crafting stories with each day.

Conversations linger, sweet and slow,
As thoughts entwine like steam in flight.
In this moment, we let go,
Whispers in the brew ignite the light.

Embrace of the Ocean

Tides pull gently at the shore,
Each wave a promise, soft and true.
In every swell, I long for more,
The ocean's heart beats just for you.

Salt and seafoam, life's embrace,
Crashing rhythms, wild and free.
Together we find our sacred space,
Beneath the sky, simply to be.

Stormy skies and clouds that weep,
Yet in their chaos, beauty thrives.
In depths unknown, our secrets keep,
Lost in the vastness, our souls revive.

Holding hands, we ride the crest,
In waters deep, our fears dissolve.
With each embrace, we are blessed,
To nature's calls, we both evolve.

The Harmony of Still Waters

Gentle ripples glide so slow,
Reflecting skies, a soft aglow.
Whispers of peace, a tranquil sigh,
Beneath the trees where shadows lie.

Morning mist caresses the lake,
Serenity's breath, no need to wake.
Birds in flight, a graceful tune,
As time dances beneath the moon.

Nature cradles its quiet heart,
In stillness lies a work of art.
Each moment captured, pure and true,
In harmony, me and you.

The world fades, it dims its light,
In this silence, all feels right.
A mirror reflects our souls' embrace,
In still waters, we find our place.

Sunsets in Every Sip

Golden hues in every glass,
Rich flavors swirl, moments pass.
With every taste, the sun dips low,
A symphony of bliss in tow.

Laughter mingles with the breeze,
Memories formed with such ease.
The twilight glows, our hearts ignite,
As day transforms to soft night light.

Each sip a journey, a story to tell,
Of sunlit pathways where dreams dwell.
To savor time, both slow and sweet,
As flavors dance, our lives complete.

In every glass, a sunset's grace,
With friends beside, we find our place.
In every drop, a spark divine,
For in these moments, we truly shine.

Savoring Serendipity

Chance encounters on winding roads,
Life unfolds, its rich episode.
Moments unexpected, fate's kind hand,
In whispers soft, make us understand.

A smile exchanged, a door swings wide,
In the unplanned, we take our stride.
Laughter ringing in cafés bright,
New friendships born in the soft twilight.

Each serendipity, a story spun,
Threads of fate in the setting sun.
Adventures waiting around each bend,
In the magic of life, love will extend.

Embrace the unknown, let worries flee,
For joy awaits in spontaneity.
In every turn, a treasure found,
In savoring life, we are unbound.

The Dance of Waves and Warmth

Waves whisper secrets to the shore,
A rhythm that beckons, forevermore.
The sun dips low, paints skies with fire,
In its warmth, hearts rise higher.

Children's laughter rides the breeze,
Footprints left on golden seas.
Shells and treasures, nature's art,
In each wave, our stories start.

As tides embrace, we join the dance,
In every splash, a fleeting chance.
To feel the pulse of ocean's sway,
In warmth and waves, we drift away.

The evening fades in hues divine,
As night embraces, and stars align.
In this moment, lost and free,
The dance of waves sings to you and me.

Morning's Embrace in a Mug

The dawn breaks softly on the day,
A warm aroma finds its way.
In the silence, dreams take flight,
Sipping slowly, hearts feel light.

The mug cradles gentle heat,
In every swirl, a rhythm sweet.
Golden rays through windows gleam,
Morning whispers of a dream.

Each taste a promise, bold and true,
In every sip, the world anew.
Wrapped in warmth, the worries fade,
In a moment's pause, peace is made.

With every breath, the day begins,
Where hope and calm, together spin.
Morning's embrace, a soft caress,
A treasure found, a quiet bliss.

Soothing Brews and Ocean Views

The waves crash softly on the shore,
With every sip, I ask for more.
A cup of warmth in ocean breeze,
Nature whispers, hearts at ease.

Steam rising, mingling with the salt,
A tranquil moment, no fault at all.
Gazing out where sea meets sky,
With every taste, the spirit flies.

Brewed perfection in a gentle hand,
A soothing balm, a timeless strand.
Together here, I feel the flow,
In every drop, serenity grows.

Soothing colors, sunset hue,
In this moment, there's only you.
The ocean sighs, the world feels right,
With every slurp, the soul takes flight.

The Calm Before Sunset

Shadows lengthen, the day holds breath,
A tranquil pause before its death.
With cup in hand, I watch the light,
As colors dance to say goodnight.

The skies ablaze in fiery gold,
In every sip, a story told.
Moments linger, sweet and slow,
A gentle warmth in evening's glow.

A world unwinds, the noise subsides,
In calm reflections, peace resides.
The final rays begin to fade,
But in this pause, hope is laid.

I hold the warmth, I feel the grace,
In twilight's touch, I find my place.
Each heartbeat whispers, soft and sweet,
In nature's calm, my soul feels complete.

Steeping in Serenity

Leaves unfurl in a simmering pot,
Time slows down, a precious knot.
With gentle swirls, the colors blend,
In every sip, I find a friend.

Fragrant steam wraps around my face,
As worries fade, I find my space.
Strength in stillness, a soothing call,
Each moment savored, I embrace it all.

The world outside may spin and race,
But here I sit in sacred grace.
Infused with calm, my heart expands,
In liquid warmth, the spirit stands.

A nightly ritual, a gentle way,
To end the hours of a busy day.
Steeping deeper, as shadows play,
In this stillness, I long to stay.

Flowing Moments in a Cup

In the morning light, it brews,
A dance of warmth, a gentle muse.
A blend of dreams, both bold and sweet,
In each spilled drop, our moments meet.

The steam ascends, a fleeting sigh,
Captured whispers of days gone by.
Each sip a journey, slow, sublime,
Time flows with grace, a tranquil rhyme.

Caffeine kisses, soft and bright,
With every taste, we take flight.
In porcelain worlds, we lose and find,
Flowing moments, hearts entwined.

As shadows dance, the sun dips low,
In this cup, our stories flow.
Memories steeped, forever won,
In every sip, we become one.

The Warmth Between Us

A quiet glance, a knowing smile,
In silence shared, we linger a while.
Your hand in mine, a tender grace,
In every touch, we find our place.

The fire flickers, casting gold,
In its embrace, our hearts unfold.
Through whispered secrets, soft and light,
The warmth between us, pure delight.

As shadows dance upon the walls,
In cozy corners, the evening calls.
Through laughter's echo, love's sweet play,
The warmth between us, here to stay.

With every heartbeat, every sigh,
A bond forged deep, we reach the sky.
In every moment, in every breath,
The warmth between us conquers death.

Harmony of Flavors and Currents

The spices blend, a fragrant tune,
Under the stars, beneath the moon.
In pots of gold, the dance begins,
A harmony of flavors spins.

Sweet and savory, tangy and bright,
Each ingredient, a pure delight.
In every bite, the world expands,
Currents flow through loving hands.

In laughter shared over warm feasts,
We savor love, embrace the least.
A table set, a bond, a cheer,
Harmony of flavors, always near.

As echoes linger, stories weave,
In every taste, we learn to believe.
Together we roam, with open hearts,
In life's vast tapestry, love imparts.

Chasing Shadows with Steam

In the cool of dusk, a kettle sings,
With every whistle, the evening brings.
Shadows dance as the daylight fades,
Chasing warmth in the twilight glades.

A cup in hand, the night divine,
With each sip, the stars align.
The quiet moments, rich and deep,
In steam's embrace, our souls will leap.

As memories rise, like clouds of grey,
We find our peace through evening's play.
Chasing shadows, the world grows still,
In steaming cups, we taste our will.

In the fading light, a tender glance,
Through swirling steam, we share our dance.
With every breath, a promise made,
Chasing shadows, in love's cascade.